The Insatiable Psalm

The Insatiable Psalm

YERMIYAHU AHRON TAUB

WIND RIVER PRESS   2005

The Insatiable Psalm
Copyright © 2005, Yermiyahu Ahron Taub

All rights reserved. No part of this book may be reproduced or transmitted in any form or by any means, electronic or mechanical, including photocopying, recording or by any information storage and retrieval system, without permission in writing from the copyright owner.

A Publication of
WIND RIVER PRESS
http://www.windriverpress.com

Hershey, Pennsylvania

Book Design: Katherine Arline
Author Photo: Grigoriy Ratinov

First Edition

Library of Congress Cataloging-in-Publication Data

Taub, Yermiyahu Ahron.
  The insatiable psalm : poems / Yermiyahu Ahron Taub.-- 1st ed.
    p. cm.
  ISBN 0-9721513-8-9
  1. Jews--Poetry. 2. Jewish families--Poetry. 3. Mothers and sons--Poetry. I. Title.
  PS3620.A895I57 2005
  811'.6--dc22
                        2005005807

IN MEMORIAM

R.T.

אין הייליקן אָנדענק

"טאַנטע" רייזי

CONTENTS

I. OUR DAYS WERE PAINTED

molly néni's song	3
immigrant eyes, averted	5
father grocer	7
invasion	8
ode from a distance	10
in the thermometer factory	12
after theory	14
lana, lost on the way	16
eye contact	17
volozhin, surpassed	18
celebration after a secret meeting with queen esther	20
ghetto noctune	22
first signs	23
one voice: rabbi's wife and friend	24
tsholnt	25
scarcity	26
picnic withheld	27
retrenchment	28
vigil	29

arrangement without sun	30
dust into stars	31
restoration rendezvous	32
passover guide	33
still life, with mirrors	35
talmudic discourse in the maternity ward	36
friday night formations	38
a house calling	40
kindergarten blues	42
instead of school	44
other tongues (in case of flight)	46
identity confirmed	47
months that flu	48
the filth box wreaks havoc!	50
to the music of melancholy	52
preparing to dance	
ENGLISH	53
YIDDISH	54
the question of moishe oysher	55
the last physical exam	57
homage restored: bar mitzvah fantasia	58
boy late to prayer	60
chocolate chip dialectic	62
kitchen espionage	64
the ladies' circle slackens	65
figure prostrate on tishah b'av stone	67

descent: internal excursion in the second person	68
east central european paradigms	70
answers on the respite banks	72
in praise of hope and honeydew	74
questions of dress	75
suggested retirement	77
iris outside time	78
despite virtue	79
insulin mikveh	80
invitation to psalm	82
caravaggio's latest boy	84
issue, hovering	86
night of awe	87
don't relinquish glamour, child	89
post parade ceremony: pride day, 199-	91
advice	93
prediction: bowery yom kippur	94
croquis in dust and shadow	95
medical breakthrough	96
the patriarch's power	97
current affairs	98
culinary miracle	99
under linen trees, whispers	100
and from there to water	102
before and after introduction	104
implications of bread	105

II. ARCHAEOLOGY OF SUGAR: METHODS

way of the footnote	109
woman of letters	110
owning the terrain of detail	111
memorandum to the beleaguered graduate student	113
women at the barricades	115
in the attic, on the ocean floor	117
notes from another tradition	118
red ink, white space	119
in the quick already gone	121
the other woman	122
negotiation suspended	124
the earliest review	125
silk tabernacle	127
sandscape	128
expanded empire	129
political funeral	130
by the grave: 'historian' and craft	131
behind siesta eyes	133
the unforsaken	135
Glossary	137
Acknowledgments	139

The Insatiable Psalm

POET'S NOTES

Although some of these poems draw upon elements of remembered experience, none should be considered strictly biographical or autobiographical.

Yiddish terms used in the book, including those of Hebrew origin, are transliterated according to the system established by the YIVO Institute for Jewish Research. Terms accepted into English follow the spelling of *Webster's Third New International Dictionary*.

I.

OUR DAYS WERE PAINTED

molly néni's song

on marcy avenue the rains came,
and two girls emerged to investigate.
through open fingers they felt
the presence of ghosts they had
only chattered about in periods of study.
one had saucers for hands,
pooled swords of porcelain, really,
brimming with candy corn.
at first, the girls simply admired the candy colors –
the orange and yellow alluded
to the tiles on molly néni's kitchen walls
and that october holiday
that sometimes brought pagan children to their door.
soon they began to reach against melting,
a crescendo of sweetness on the brink of dispersion.
to heighten their search, blue daisies came,
perhaps also to light their way.
and green fingers of little women
shook back and forth.
dazed by the sudden transparency of their need,

the girls paused and looked at each other.
and remembering the outcome of delicacies
long ago reached for,
they lifted the hems of their nightgowns and fled,
two specks of white framed by curtains so blue,
into fields of corn of just one color.

immigrant eyes, averted

we lived in small places,
sure.
the dangers (the fiery puddles all around)
dotted the streets;
we had long been warned of their persistence.
but we could also let go, drink deep.
you see, this is how it was:
stories of supreme flying men and tenor-spirited
detectives could enter,
if not through the living room,
then over the wail of summer infant
and the fire escape
and into the bedroom.
over potatoes and purple orbs,
we laughed at the broadcast solutions
that promised to lift up our shoulders and
whisk away all burdens.
also – the snaking rhythms of the orchestras,
the girls with the good news, although we never saw
their legs.

sometimes we even pondered the meaning
of baking soda.
all of these temptations of the new land
left traces on the hands of mother and father.
but their eyes remained focused,
sought to rest only in dimly lit interiors.
and in those eyes,
in our own reflections,
we saw their determination and
the mysterious rise of our faith.

father grocer

it was on the corner,
where he enacted our livelihood,
literally.
in jar of can and row of cane, days were painted.
not in muted sepia, as today, but in tones of
necessity.
flour poured forth from wells of dust,
boxes sighed in ancient knowing,
and forearms of hardworking men gleamed
in fast power. women came to arrange feasts
for the most attentive of lords and
girls to study.
presiding over all, ensuring the surest transaction,
he stood in creases of welcome.
in a time of rumor, he made certainty.
in days of destruction, he brought the driest of goods
to incandescence.

invasion

for Isabella Leitner

on the hottest day, they came.
hard women, with bright and cunning ways.
survivors of something too big to even consider,
refugee cousins from the charred remains
of a continent
i had heard too much about.
that one there, with her red nails
and red dresses and red lips and red eyes.
her smoke knifing
through the aroma of roast chicken.
and the sisters, the other ones,
fondling the brows of the men
with the white teeth and the vacant smiles,
the pages and pages of them, week after week.
once below, a sailor.
and the music, the way they paraded that staccato
over the ebb of our ways,
our days of quiet and service.

the way their numbered arms
sneered at me,
a girl coming into devotion
and a life ripe with old pears.
as if their selves had been emptied
over there into a cesspool
of mockery and lewdness.
martyrs, they might have been,
but in our enforced silence,
we knew them as lawless invaders and
beseeched them away.

ode from a distance

Boris Thomashevsky (1868-1939),
star of the Yiddish theater

he was really before me, you should know.
they all were.
but listen, i heard plenty –
from starlets on frontscapes
who dangled themselves from yellow playbills and
remembered stories of riot and grace.
the shock of the men and women in costume,
cavorting as if the purim play could be presented
all year around, endured far beyond their day.
and later, all this that had preceded me
came to adorn the walls of my late late youth.
who could resist you?
his rabbis in crisis, princes in abandon
drew lines of anticipation and expectation.
so that carriages of milk and silk
were forced to consider their options anew.
with boys on our arms and aunts two rows ahead,

we suspended fear and slid, however briefly,
into hours of rapture and moments
of carefully distilled groping.
and though i and the later girls
would come to look upon men who had moved out
west and uptown,
i always summoned him, the one i had never seen.
before sleep i always knew i could ensure his return
by beginning to reconfigure the trail of petals
he once scattered in my book of daily prayer.

in the thermometer factory

was it good to have income,
did you dream of two plain rooms in the city.
maybe with a girlfriend in tailored suits
who would sometimes slow down to tell you all.
maybe alone, where you would gather the fruits
of worship and weave them through
your darkening curls.
did you think study could not last,
that your life was too far from the center of the plague.
did you think maybe teacher's seminary.
only perhaps a little later,
but first this.
with your wages, did you buy that severe number
(that i spotted in a snapshot of what looked
like a nightclub),
buried now in mothballs.
or maybe you saved only for the future,
for the imminent outbreak of cholera.
as the day grew longer,
as the voices modulated their 5 o'clock anticipation,

did you think i'm just biding my time.
one more pinch on the buttocks,
just one more mercury shower,
and then he is bound to appear.

after theory

and i came from crowded one rooms,
shoulders bowed in attention to industry and hunger.
barks of bulging men with determined
rows of numbers
over their heads and lazy nimble fingers squeezing
curves too slow and afraid roaring in my eyes,
i saw no other way.
but here were bodies pushing forward and profiles
illuminated in rage and method.
talking low against encroaching exhaustion,
they rejected the minutiae of possession
and declared a sharp and terrifying present.
first i imagined only texts,
this was the way i had fought to know.
then strategies exploded and i saw
that bodies would fall.
later i would come to question
and still later to longevity.
now i wore only determination
and dressed quickly for my tasks

of looking and concealing.
and you placed a hand upon my crown of dark braids.

lana, lost on the way

sacred man, how did you get your face so radiant.
if i touch it, will my prints wring scars.
may i?
in its deep hollows, however,
i feel sure i will find the right words.
your ears stand so tucked away, barely there,
undisturbed by the elusive rhythms i have so needed.
the benny goodman days are over.
and judging by our courtship,
i will have to hurry now,
fever to engrave:
arms outstretched against the coney island heavens
on a film of the most brittle cotton candy.
when will i see lana t. again?
sacred man, crown rabbi,
i know the work will never end.
i know too that i can never attain your gleam,
but please accept that i am prepared for this surrender.

eye contact

everyone came, people she hardly
remembered knowing.
as if this was the final appearance
of a disintegrating soprano
or the banquet of a diplomat on a fat mission to woo
post-colonial investment. only instead,
it was the beginning of a young woman's new life.
long tables of food anchored the choreographed joy
of alliances pursued, of a nation furthered,
of a family forged, of the longevity of unification
embodied in the expanse of one vast gown.
feet moved in circles that grew small and fast,
always careful to support
the moat of white shielding her.
and for a while, they succeeded.
but when her veil was lifted,
she looked into the eyes of God and saw that,
as if after a final bout of weeping,
all the tenderness was gone.

volozhin, surpassed

in those early days,
we were pioneers battling on the tundra
of the brahmin elite.
not that we ever saw them –
too busy was he with the minds
of the young sages-in-training
and i with the imagined specifics of their bodies.
although he did not miss a fine pair
of broad shoulders
and i occasionally conversed on topics
other than meat stew.
rows of dark and white huddled over the bowls of
whatever slop i chose to inflict –
vats of remains yawning in the galley behind them,
awaiting their fate.
mess hall!
sometimes i would enchant with a vacant grin.
usually i was too exhausted to make out anything
other than their endless commitment and my own
conviction that this experiment could not survive,

that, even after Volozhin,
the yeshivah founders had underestimated
the force of the new england chill.

celebration after a secret meeting with queen esther

at the descent of the guillotine,
we will be transformed,
in the folk idiom.
without woodcuts and lithographs,
though with no shortage of possibility.
you see, the doorbell did not stop,
seemed frozen in climax.
gifts poured in.
let it all out.
let it be known far and wide:
the pogrom has been averted!
so that the students,
lithe and expectant,
adam's apples bobbing with spirit,
cheered and hollered.
so that she threw her head back,
so that her long neck gleamed
in the palm of the early dark
and the youths perspired in a bliss of admiration.
o rabbi's wife, how did haman get so far?

so that she crossed her legs,
i don't know, boys,
passed vodka all around, drew closer the circle,
and opened the night profuse:
but draw near and let me tell you
what was whispered at the queen's dusk,
let me tell you what i learned
the night i got news of the reprieve ...

ghetto nocturne

no rooms rented by the week,
no concierge bitter with extension.
hookers and sailors never stop here,
though dry humping is sometimes heard.
drunks don't stagger against alley walls;
though sometimes they dress in smile.
no silhouette illuminated by blue neon;
these players do not require visibility.
no muffling of steel by sinew tearing,
no laughter knifing through the night.
outside the gates of the quarter,
no movement.
the skies buckle with absence;
the gutters perspire with moan.

first signs

when did the glimpse become shimmer.
as you moved through the corridor
on the road to light the sabbath furnace,
bent to remove the last defiant stain.
maybe in mid-bend?
on the highway from the rooms,
near the dance hall,
did you gasp from the strength of my thrusts.
did you hear footsteps growing from the distance,
or did my tread, my approach come upon you
all at once.
suddenly there,
drunk and prepared for your bright dark prayer.

one voice: rabbi's wife and friend

    this requirement that can come to love,
    the marriage of duty and rapture.
    when we awaken to cries of unidentifiable need.
    when we struggle to stave off shadows lurking
    and demons that feast upon tender flesh.
    when white cloth filled with burning stench
    assails the air in a gust that no longer
    reeks only of pragmatism.
    when suckle releases only dull milk
    and we feel that these years can never end.
    when on the occasions of rupture,
    (when hooded messengers shuffle through and away
    and evenings can never be the same),
    then, only then,
    will we remember the insatiable nights of origin.

tsholnt

❧

>you must note the perfect pallor of
>those potatoes,
>the persistent wink of the yam,
>the round green of the outer onion,
>the cloves that traveled far
>from the caves of former colonies
>to seduce the most elusive of flanks,
>the list that cannot explain the way
>the chef was driven,
>the whimsical grin of the divine.

scarcity

    the entire campaign is dependent upon deployment.
    table scrubbed white of stain,
    drained of all impurity.
    soup hot and mellow,
    calm after its long simmer.
    chicken: tenderness heightened in garlic
    only just beginning to stagnate under the white candle.
    a child's knuckles white in expectation.
    a man stroking the force of sanctity.
    a woman nursing watermelon unpurchased.
    and pear compote turned into war rations.

picnic withheld

even if he insisted on tomorrow,
it could never have been enough.
today was so rich, so ripe with planning.
the plains of coffee burning under the
eclipse. my new dress white and gossamer
with longing. the shoes black but elongated
with practicality,
made for fields of yellow and purple flower.
what are they called?
sweetheart, those flowers, what did you say
they were called?
it was simply a day that seemed to beckon, to
insist, one might say, upon extravagance.
what happened in the end –
sudden unavailability, added preparation for a lecture –
was something that i know could have been undone.
something that should have become expectation
not dashed,
but simply unimagined.

retrenchment

you'll see, it won't be so bad.
we'll stay here and smash the day to joy.
we'll make pictures of ogres with brittle black beards,
then we'll shave them and use them to scour the toilets.
we'll make bonfires of hats of men who refuse the
brocade of the leisured afternoon.
then we'll rest and make
marble cake for the day after tomorrow.
it's going to be o.k. he'll come soon,
sniffing the ashes of our fires, he'll plea for reprise.
he won't begin from the beginning,
but he'll see the importance
of food spread lavishly over a place of green. suddenly,
this small pleasure will cause meaning.
together you and i will force bouquets of white tulips
to appear alongside tense talmudic dispute.
and you will breathe again.

vigil

i made vacation bungalows for my dolls,
though no one could see them.
my fat bear can be so still that
only we can hear him breathe.
i gorged on oatmeal raisin cookie
and was struck by the pallor left on my tongue.
when i drew the house on the hill, clouds threatened,
and so i hurried to witness their arrival.
the storm that greeted me still seemed only an idea,
an imitation of impending doom,
a reference to something we had read about together.
so i did what i should have done at the outset
and began my long ascent.
by the foot of the domed quiet,
i stood with my candle and prayed
that this trip would be shorter than the others.

arrangement without sun

in the eras of maternal dark,
the roots had to be guarded.
no one could question the strange path of their thirst.
in a fog of familiarity yet devoid of insight,
they all knew how to counter the paralysis of air.
children got busy.
they discovered projects abandoned for years:
drawers to be evacuated; photographs to be perused,
avoided, and arranged;
a bowl to be filled with dapper fruit
and suddenly brought to bear upon
an unsuspecting end table;
traces of velvet to restrain curtains from themselves.
creativity spent, the children would inevitably
return to the mundane,
not without fear. would their actions be misinterpreted?
their work seen as derision or accusation?
how would they know until it was all over?
terrified of the outcome,
the children put aside the mops and sponges
and slunk into dark rooms of their own.

dust into stars

who are all these little ones,
descended upon me from up north,
wrung from my fickle womb.
what are they looking for and what can i give?
once i knew the meaning of day without night.
i could coax silence from the most stubborn wail.
my touch was renowned.
now i stay with surface and response that i can foresee.
with polish i fight the demons of disintegration and
create tapestries of dustlessness.
only in this scoured sweep can i
reach the expanse of comfort
that beckons to me over the kerchief
of my hunched neighbor.
i offer no apologies; this is what is best.
listen, it is good to see so many familiar faces.
but this is hardly the place for you and
these strange and unprepared children.

restoration rendezvous

come in. don't be scared.
it's still me. come here and sit.
there's plenty of room.
how have you been all these days?
so long and thin you seem.
did you eat all that you promised?
you must keep up your strength.
orange juice is so good, such a gift.
i had to stay in here for a while,
but i fell asleep with you.
soon i'll be back.
in no time.
i just need a little more sleep.
sometimes, out in the other rooms, i get tired.
no, shh.
come up here.
of course this is hard.
later on, some day, you'll see,
i'll prove to you that i have more to give than this.

passover guide

over the evolving array of green and silver,
mother saw bird of another kind.
only there was much to be arranged:
delicacies to celebrate a liberation
that insisted upon blood and frogs
but related more to feasts of recent eras.
the end results, that is,
the ones that had once been assured,
appeared entirely unattainable.
despite the abundance of discipline,
mortar appeared flaky,
was too much about nuts.
herbs threatened to be bitter for entirely other reasons.
and salt water had proved entirely unnecessary.
still, redemption had to proceed.
the bread had to be hurried,
the slaves had to revise their relationship to the sun,
the places of life and love had to be forever dispelled.
amidst this delirium of activity,
during the briefest upward glance

mother spotted an unknown bird,
saw how unfazed it was by the lack of leftover
and quickly warned it to stay away.
yet though it heard her warning,
the bird could not abandon the cry of her arms
and the power of her finger work.
she heard the reassuring sweep of its wings
as it guided her through
the shouts of the others
and the parting of the sea.

still life, with mirrors

behold the absence of slime,
but don't underestimate the forces
that sought this eradication.
take note of the ways in which local foliage
embraces touch.
if you observe with care,
you will see yourself in the same glass
through which books now sparkle
with some degree of ease.
and you will want to see yourself here,
in this house of learning.
you will feel yourself expanded by this place,
by the intimacy forged by such ancient knowing.
and though you must set aside time to absorb it all,
it is not wise to dawdle.
on the contrary, it is best to move quickly.
don't consider the silence to be an assurance.
don't see the sealed doors as corridors to a greeting.

talmudic discourse in the maternity ward

on this there is only assent,
an unparalleled quiet.
never before has she seen so many united faces,
nodding heads.
their beards enclose her in a chain of certainty.
hats askew,
they assure that the commandment pertains
only to him,
to them.
except that through her help (vessel? vassal?),
she too is guaranteed a berth
in the eternal configuration,
which, in the end, is all she has ever wanted.
i have not been summoned to negotiate, she argues.
nor we to grant the inadmissible, they remind:
you are not a receptacle, but a joyous participant.
in your work, by skirting the literal,
you redefine the very question of means.
the production of the body, whether successful or not,
cannot alter the edicts the body receives from above.

the struggle for production must continue. yes?
this will be your solace.
so she is informed in the zone of bleached
light and inadequate pajama.
yet after the quarantine of expectation,
mother cannot determine the relevance
of these conversations.
only later will their lesson will be absorbed and heeded.
now she wants to know the source
of the inaudible cries,
the methods for securing the stains wrought
by the bloodied bundles of flesh –
can they be brought to stay?
against the blurred movement of visitor,
she wants only to touch the nurse's hands,
to caress the contours of their emptiness.

friday night formations

two women sway under a great shade,
speaking of times immemorial.
though long tucked away and deep down,
their hair expands under the approval
of the newly arrived sabbath empress.
the silhouette of their words brings contentment:
bread braided in exquisite control.
castles arranged in a burst of bearded vigor
and a gown pressed from the most nuanced chiffon.
then tales of the newly arrived in the most
ghastly steerage.
if you must know –
twelve furious pounds of persistence –
were we ever that eager?
maybe the potion, the one descended
from the knuckles of garlic,
could have eased the toil of release, the tearing of walls
and the first moment of life that we never,
even in the lost lost times, forget.
yet never a mention of the hands that raked

the ravages of restlessness and the persistence of dust
and leaped, stunned, into pools
of black water and reunion.
never.
only words of rest and the rustling of a shadow
of a boy,
who in long white skirts of his own,
wonders when all of this will be his.

a house calling

in a mansion of nineteenth-century medicine,
site of unimpeachable respectability and folly,
an old game is replayed.
it's far away, of course, where it has to be,
where it can only be. under the eaves,
in the attic, maybe. only you know.
there, two children move into a vision
of taut transformation.
unravel go polyester pants and white ritual cotton
and smooth pale harps and clavicle are revealed.
sister, come with me.
help me with the folds of this impossible
turban. careful with the rhinestones.
tell me what to do with silk tunic:
are its long yellow lines enough for tonight,
this one and only night?
and of this skirt, when the men return
from shul, what will they know?
all the children in the world
and still such a woman.

tonight, they'll have to see for themselves.
will it be clear, big sister?
come, this once, let's go down
and see what mother thinks.

kindergarten blues

she said it would be great fun,
that turquoise and purple turtles would change
the way i interpreted trees.
rhododendron would leap from walls
and caress corduroy jumpsuits.
circles of movement would enfold me
so that my newly learned song
would levitate the shopping malls.
and later i would have to tell her all that i had seen.
yet none of this came to pass.
snowflakes strewn about and aplenty –
ceiling, doors, windows –
threatened to smother me in a blizzard of listlessness.
instead of color i saw only cheer.
that is: others similarly displaced
but determined to make the best of things.
ugh.
or else: outraged and thus banished to the corner.
i grew small and grim:
so this is how it was going to be!

under the quiver of the teacher's assistant,
i found a crayon and
began to sketch this spectacular tableau of betrayal.

instead of school

children, gather your things and remember.
it's time you knew of such things.
our journey may be brief
but your attention must be constant.
don't lose these papers.
you will need them to cross into the neighboring region.
a thousand clouds will be forced
to stifle our locomotive's wail.
so we should have plenty of rest.
peering into our cars will be the flattened faces
of the well-heeled.
pay them no mind. it isn't really us
they're watching, anyway.
listen, when we disembark, we will be
in a rocky terrain,
with just a few scrub pines.
and there may be some pandemonium.
we may even get momentarily separated. stay wily.
you will be asked who are you,
where do you come from.

you may answer these questions in part or completely.
whatever you do, though, be sure not to tell them
that you traveled with me.

other tongues (in case of flight)

don't forget your irregular verbs,
yet don't draw attention with perfection.
strip it all down: get a handle on the conversational;
harness the command mode.
don't think of the confusion at the station –
the pandemonium of fog, the dance of smoke,
the blanket of bone.
but take heed of the ephemeral signs.
this cannot be overemphasized.
there won't be time later,
everything will move too fast.
so now, before it is too late,
dazzle me with your new conjugations.

identity confirmed

don't be fooled by the false curls,
by the breasts lightly spread.
the skirts, black and flowing, may seem appropriate.
and you've seen the apartment:
everything is in its place.
a sofa here, a chair there.
on the mantle, a figurine.
even the papers,
you've shuffled through them a thousand times;
have seen a thousand others.
you would know, if anyone would,
if everything is in order. it's all fairly routine.
the cunning they have come to display:
the shrewdness of prey.
it cannot endure.
let it be known.
let there be no cause for doubt:
this is definitely the one.

months that flu

the cards came pouring in,
missives of fourth grade well-wishing.
balloons green and profuse over
meadows of beagle under greetings
vague and befuddled:
friend, hope you feel better.
p.s. what exactly is wrong?
after a glance we tossed them atop my bureau,
marveling at my sudden visibility.
then we thought we'd close the shades and take
care of the business at hand: my tepid brow.
mother leaped under the deep cover and
applied cool compress, while i giggled at the droplets
streaming down the hollows of my chest
and made room for the bed of head stubble
she lowered across my left nipple.
mother announced she absolutely had to report
that she had heard that somebody had said
that only earnestness brings cure.
which made us roll and roll in glee

until we had to clutch each other for reprieve.
and so we began to rock together.
until mother whispered,
i feel the fever losing its hold,
soon the color will diminish,
what will become of us when you go back?

the filth box wreaks havoc!

when we welcomed great aunt,
we knew she was bringing
more than a chest full of brown photographs
and those woody scones we had heard so much about.
and this knowledge seasoned
over the two years of her stay.
you see, there it stood: in silence a wooden box
with a sealed green face.
brought to life, however, it became
explosive with sound.
wait! not so fast! this ritual required its
own preparation.
first, father had to be diverted with holy task.
but also great aunt had to be buried
in albums and envelopes.
only then could children enter the world of
*goingsteadymakingoutcheerleaderpracticegeebobbycap
tainoffootballteamnerd*
and other exotica banal and mesmerizing.
you see, when jan dreamed of marcia's fall,

we too were affected.
we knew that something had to be done.
and so gradually mother came to sin.
with us it was to smile with indulgence.
but soon it was the two women upstairs alone.
and sulking, we were forced to rely upon hearsay
of revenge and lust and burning antebellum mansions.
and then even this changed.
spying through the keyhole into the hall of instant cash
(if only the tune could be named),
we grew quiet as mother named them all,
golden oldies and big bands
and crooners so smooth we thought
we would never stop sliding.
here crouched a vast encyclopedic repertoire,
a compilation of impure erudition
that had no relationship
to the daily exhibition of housecoat and psalm.
i squeezed sister's hand and looked
across an abyss at a woman
who had dreamed of night clubs
and may even have seen tuxedoes.
and i thought who is this woman?
she can't possibly stay.

to the music of melancholy

embellishment stood uncertain by the carved door.
the bareness gave such comfort. everyone was away,
no one in preparation.

*take my hand like this, a woman like me has never
needed an opportunity.
i was born knowing the mystery of movement.
a boy like you – years of keeping the musicians company –
take my shoulder against that light.
fingers, forever nimble, will allow no pause.
and you won't need it. dip your hand below the curve.
show me that you see. circle the couch,
sense its upcoming bulk.
pause knowingly around the shrews.
take me to an implausible sky.*

mother grows weary of improbability,
and we remember the time.
and the trail of silver light hardens the vein
in the wall above her now quieted shoulder.

preparing to dance

    she sits on the chair in a sea
    of the palest pink,
    floating.
    the *sheytl* (blonder
    than the now darkened braid packed
    away in the drawer),
    an open fist.
    mother looks into the glass,
    long.
    without a sigh
    she applies the red and the blue,
    scent from an unmarked bottle,
    camouflage of things unknown.
    the pearls in place,
    she lowers her head onto the desk,
    her shoulders shaking,
    unable to budge the man's words from below.
    and the little boy stares through the lace
    in awe.

צוגרייטנדיק צו טאַנצן

❧

זי זיצט אויף אַ בענקל אין אַ ים פֿון
דער בלייכסטער ראָזקייט,
שווימענדיק.
דאָס שייטל (בלאָנדער
ווי דער איצט פֿאַרטונקלטער צאָפּ באַהאַלטן
אינעם שופֿלאָד),
אַן אָפֿענע פֿויסט.
די מאַמע קוקט אינעם גלאָז,
לאַנג.
אָן אַ זיפֿץ,
לייגט זי צו דאָס רויט און בלוי,
בשׂמים-ריח פֿון אַן אומבאַצייכנטע פֿלעשל,
קאָמופֿלאַזש פֿאַר זאַכן אומבאַוווּסטע.
די פּערל אין אָרדענונג,
לאָזט זי אַראָפּ דעם קאָפּ אויפֿן טיש,
מיט צידערדיקע אַקסלען,
נישט אין שטאַנד אַ ריר צו טאָן דעם מאַנס ווערטער
פֿון אונטן.
און דאָס קליינע ייִנגל פֿאַרקוקט זיך אַדורך די שפּיצן
מיט אָפּשי.

the question of moishe oysher

1.
aretha's beat slithers through me
transforming me into the sexy bar mitzvah diva
i know myself to be.
"such filth, such garbage,
not in this house!!" mother, avoiding metaphor,
suddenly screeches.
then as quickly "please, please."
with a terrible finality, knowing the way from here,
i pronounce:
"aretha is not negotiable."

2.
surrounded by the crazy sunday morning potpourri
of mordechai ben david and the barry sisters,
only this time it's moishe oysher.
mother throws back her neck, lifts her
dishwashy fists to her chest,
turns to me: "have you ever heard such a voice?"
my "no, I haven't" emerges from the doorway,

where i remain rooted.
so that years later,
when i hear the extended elegiac refrains
and the calls for respect,
i always take care to change the station.

the last physical exam

    let me look at you,
    at the strong man you're becoming.
    at those bones expanding into
    unforeseen frame.
    at the hair flourishing wiry in all those distant places
    that i have known and understood.
    at the arms whose sinew i memorized
    on a tapering july night.
    at the nipples that once quivered beneath
    the drying white ridges of mine.
    and at the lips that will lead you
    into alien and demanding embrace.

homage restored: bar mitzvah fantasia

    in my reservoir of preparatory dread,
    i chose not to see. so intent on
    retention and self-preservation,
    no thought even to gorgeous ancient words.
    (get it down, boy.)
    this time, flight to the third floor
    would be out of the question.
    (the moment of inscription is upon you.
    don't look around.)
    only now can i glimpse
    the tables laden with grandeur
    and the assembled famished for your genius.
    even flush with my small escape and the
    torpor derived from oblivious strangers,
    i can still hurry down,
    for once clear of my task
    to the kitchen side/to the women's section,
    to take your hands in mine, to whisper:
    all this you have orchestrated.
    here, by the table of your peers,

i bow in honor of this intricate work
and in thanks for this lavish welcome.

boy late to prayer

boy late to prayer
wanders over dust and once wood,
unsure of his step, unsure of reason,
knowing only the way to release.
woman stirs under the silk of sleep.
boy removes the impediments,
hearing the sway and the moaning
of the men in the sacred hall,
comes to understand the rhythms he will need.
woman reaches for the signs below her window.
run, boy, run.
the scroll has been read and still he cannot finish.
where others stream in and out,
leaving only their stench,
he will stay to summon all the hunger
he can manage in this eternal squatting position.
he will perfect the vision of divine muscle,
the gods of arm that bend further and further away.
so that boy unfinished absent from prayer
must hurry down the street,

mindful of the women on the road to preparation,
to the porch window to see the woman
complete the sabbath egg salad.
boy crouches by the bushes near the front door.
woman stirs, unsure of what she has heard,
shaking against the cobweb step of the visitor
and the traces of his breath which
stain the window behind her.

chocolate chip dialectic

I.
no blood concealed within.
no stain or secret,
dash of gothic,
not even a pinch of those.
these confections cannot be interpreted.
they were wrought by hand
in an oven without blame,
propelled by yeast without surprise.
do you still want them?

II.
smooth and unvexed,
don't be deceived.
beneath cream lurks sweat.
under the chips crouch splinters.
sometimes crumbs of longing
are tossed into the batter.
don't burn your fingers!
most of all, be patient.

only the head housekeeper holds the key to the freezer.
and there's a long process of application.

kitchen espionage

in this formula was contained the steady
momentum of creation.
i wondered what defined its generosity,
the way it heightened a dizzy awareness.
sources had informed me that my competitor
had sent her daughter to the grocer
and then banished her from the laboratory.
but i knew to speculate about grains
and droplets of things –
the nature of sugar and vanilla –
and to conceal the necessity of moist walls.
at this point, on the brink of the eggs,
i imagined her as she twisted the predicted.
here, she would remove the batter
and inject her miraculous venom.
i saw her at this moment, conjured her artistry.
i, whose skill with consistency, was not unknown,
was forced to pause over my own bowl of now slop,
the treasure only one step away,
and await the announcement of her triumph.

the ladies' circle slackens

all my talk, who have i fooled.
the mantle of my rabbinical spousal
respectability twitching,
nylons all run on game shows.
still, i partook.
not always in the intricacy of organization,
but in appearance.
i've long mastered the uses of a strategically placed nod.
amazing, its importance, its sufficiency.
my reward: the anticipation of the moment
when i could close the curtain of my cave,
lean my head against the wood,
savor the heat of release
and return to the pleasure of my carefully
honed diffusion.
eventually i would have to re-emerge
to once again face the sea of wigs of the neighborhood
arbiters of fate,
but now i had all i needed.
no link was ever broken,

no snag, however thick, that could not be repaired.
of course i never fooled anyone,
but then no one seemed to want to be the wiser, either.

figure prostrate on tishah b'av stone

while the second temple burned,
while the jews huddled in lament,
mother stared into a smaller flame.
even in the narrow of the last august rain,
the flame soared persistent into beads
of corn and careful salmon:
the feast after the fast.
its concentration refused to be touched by the
return of men who collapsed into sticky beds
and napped under the maps of their blank hunger.
and as the surrounding flames against the edifice
grew more furious,
and the desecration more lurid – pigs and swastikas –
mother found she had to put the food aside,
to forego the solitary light.
she had to hurry to shelter by the side of the road,
under the kitchen table.
she needed to lie prostrate,
biting into the wooden columns,
in order to avoid the oncoming hooves
of the terrified horses.

descent: internal excursion in the second person

you would have walled yourself against the bodies,
clung to the shards of your father's teenage era.
slow slow would you have redescended into
the fantasies of a world that you would never have left.
"ice cream" in coffee on a round marble table
    after *gimnazye*
your obsession sure to continue under a corner of sun
    on one obscure day.

in the rattle of the cattle cars you saw the accordion
    of the street
musicians sob unheard by all except your
    pedestal father and
then clatter back onto the back of the reluctant monkey.
even this seemed planned, though we needed the music.
Oh, how your other father, the rabbi democrat,
    needed the music!
in that metal clatter you would have summoned
    the will, only the good

of a man connected to a propaganda
    of the highest deed that
could only have found possibility in those
    skin tight coalitions.
leftcenterleftrightcenterright
centercenter
nights fraught with pliable plutocrats
    surrounded by smoke
and stubborn daughters in muslin on a cloud

of longing and devotion. even at its thwarted pinnacle,
the day would have welcomed the approach of rest,
    secure in the
fruition of its seemingly inevitable successor.
    you would not have seen
the graffiti and the defeated shops,
    would have refused their meaning.
you would have dug deeper, entrenched us all,
    would have seen your sky tarnished,
burnt before you let go. slow slow
    would you have descended far

so that the clouds of carnage would have remained
    mere wreaths in the distance
so that you, whore, would never have reached
    your just destination.

east central european paradigms

so that i came to rest against the brunt
of impossible standard.
you see, it seemed so fleeting.
yet i witnessed its weekly occurrence;
it was sustained.
father would ascend with a silver tray
and offer treasures from the nearby city.
i remember design:
swirls of brown and layers of cream.
maybe bread, how can i be sure?
definitely fruit: oranges, always pears, once kiwi.
mother would extend her calves,
rearrange her cotton fortress with rebirth.
in this way father would transform the
afternoon into holiness.
and thus mother allowed herself to return.
so that i now,
peering into the masks of these increasingly
dense sacred manuals,
must lower my eyes from the flood

of that distant union,
turn my ears away from the haze
of your grandparents' holiday laughter.

answers on the respite banks

mother tucks herself back into silk bowl.
from there she will crisp the ingredients of black
that she has assembled.
everything must be right for this occasion.
sensible shoes will complete her readiness.
the rabbi of her youth,
on recess from questions of knives
and shattered chicken necks,
must not be distracted.
fumbling with her buttons,
she vows to map the situation.
once by his brook, she will release all blame.
near the fawns that he has devoted to know,
an acknowledgment of the weight of her struggle
will be allowed.
she will separate herself from the heat
of youthful certainty,
from the battle of nuptial talmudics that she can hear
even in the suite of her summer flight.
the rabbi will comment on peace of household

and the fragility of newly hatched young wings.
and she will know what to do.
mother ties the kerchief under her chin
and makes her way down the ladder
to the ears of the delicate forest.

in praise of hope and honeydew

we will never know what we will discover.
we must be prepared, alert.
green shell will not narrow our adventure
for inside lies dough, delicious in possibility.
under the awning of cold space,
you may not detect the future.
but here everything will open.
we will peel and see ourselves rejoined.
no manuals will be consulted,
though others have certainly tread similar paths.
this could be our sublime day.
it is impossible to foresee
if leaves of gold will unfold before our pale eyes
or if we will learn the way of the light to enduring red.
perhaps we will come to understand
the vines of persistence
that still flourish in the gaps between our convictions.
i want you only to lay aside your tome.
come, not to drain the flesh,
but to replenish the sources of forgiveness.

questions of dress

    what comes of dresses unpurchased,
    of dazzle left in the window.
    after years of cartwheels in
    the midnight kitchen
    and agility wrenched from pennies,
    against the frantic cries for the essential toy
    and a dervish in the room next door
    braced against the siren dance of the material,
    what are their chances?
    what happens to a certainty of seeing,
    an insistence on lavender and lime
    never brought to touch,
    never laid to restore against depleted skin.
    do these dresses simply remain
    motionless in boutiques, distant
    but still somehow nourishing for the mere
    momentary rush.
    or do they grow wings,
    able to broadcast far and long
    a message of condemnation of the will

that rejected them
and settled instead for a procession of platitude.

suggested retirement

of course blue suits you.
you know it always has.
the lines are severe but not without integrity.
look, this is a practical garment.
under its awning you have guarded the porch.
between its folds you have ruled a minor empire.
we, in turn, have witnessed how
your upper body has slowly rearranged itself
to the remains of its form.
and that your skin, once so unclaimed,
has assumed the hue of its protector.
to its insistent devotion,
we pay this dress our muted homage.
but, darling, it too is tired.
it must be put to rest.

iris outside time

from the market no clouds by the window.
she secures the meat and milk
in their allotted ground.
and the beans away from danger.
for the end she unveils three irises and
frames them with the diminishing afternoon.
the song of the refrigerator accompanying
the removal of her shopping shoes,
mother opens her psalm.
before beginning the chapter of the day,
she allows her gaze to caress the flowers.
in that fleeting moment,
their stems rise unadorned;
their crowns expand,
unfettered by questions of indulgence
or the din of memory.

despite virtue

    she was so matter-of-fact.
    this is what a married woman must relinquish.
    this is what is done, no more and no less.
    so she would sometimes assert when she
    had to scratch her head,
    straighten her kerchief, or remove her wig
    after a service,
    eager to be freed of the headgear's weight,
    if not its meaning.
    once freed, the locks, evenly ravaged, somehow shone.
    filaments of gold remained.
    flattened all these years and still a bounce.
    i stared; it was impossible to turn away.
    despite her repeated attempts at training,
    a life of insistence,
    mother's hair outwitted the edicts of the sages!

insulin mikveh

i never dreamed so.
to be at once burdened and yet utterly aloft.
fine grain particles flow through me,
as i look through steam at the outlines
of the other immersed.
here i bob, coated in a nightgown of sentimentality.
the very foundations for my uncluttered pastry,
once the sources for my small ghetto fame,
are now conspiring for my downfall.
all those years we had worked so well together –
i, the oven, and these particles –
truly a partnership of peers.
and then suddenly, in mid-life,
this betrayal: a coagulation that slowly
reshapes my relationship to the earth.
a small blizzard threatens to smother
everything i touch.
mighty is the step of your decision.
but, dear one, please take me back
to the previous woman.

remove this sickly saccharine dust and
restore to power the stable rule of my bitterness.

invitation to psalm

mother dives into the waters of persuasion.
the people are in terrible need.
never does she seek meaning from tribulation.
like the most stringent disciple of exterior,
she rejects the lure of interpretation.
though she would not put it quite this way.
not at all, actually.
she sees the swift incision around a burning breast,
the incipient arrival of the marrow,
the necessity for the release of stones,
the crescendo of her own sugar
as transactions,
sacrifices to a hard and exacting force
not always named.
above the book open by the tomato,
she tells the reluctant one
that the young david understood the ways of entreaty,
the power of a lowered head.
he remembered that prayer was not
bound by acceptance

but was a means of detecting the hints to a new fate.
beneath the panels of anesthesia,
anything can happen.
with so many ingredients at work,
our words can sway the outcome.
come, she says, turn the page
and join the king in lyric.

caravaggio's latest boy

(Pennsylvania Academy of the Fine Arts, 198-)

a youth swathed in soon-to-be ex-ultra
Orthodox voluptuousness
drapes still over a dozen knitted brows
and ghosts of pointillists past.
all around theories careen,
methodologies lope.
chiaroscuro?
under the canopy of pillars,
he sees the swell of his own forbidden
buttock against expanses of saffron satin.
observing, he suddenly observes:
arms outstretched,
grapes flowering between nipples,
crushed irises bursting forth from penis leaves.
the calls for naturalism —
a heralding of the nineteenth-century
boxers and rowers
and oaths of loyalty to place —

are not thrown out of the academic windows;
they're simply not heeded.
it's this boy –
all those commandments long branded
between the eyes.
and limbs only just being seen – what can we say?
can you see the invisible?
the precision of this scene must be made apparent:
the bold have assembled to trace the beginning
of something as yet undetermined,
to formulate the configuration of brinkness.
here, limbs embrace light and bones open
to the most rigorous of commentary.
only the spine,
the students sketch,
still shivers under its inability to maintain blankness.

issue, hovering

what did you imagine. how did you read
the signs to the obvious.
on the summer breeze the way i moved into decision.
how i understood the vagaries of lavender and gray
as you floundered in a delicious haze of uncertainty.
when i insisted the seder plate had to stand alone
in its own discrete splendor.
that's the word i used back then: d-i-s-c-r-e-t-e.
(after p.t.a., did you emerge with
new knowledge of my jump rope cool.
did you see the envy in my eye as i forged
the braid of sister).
when you watched me flit around the room
with a towel whirling pink as if music was soaring
and i the featured ballerina.
as you turned the pages of the *tkhines*,
there was no awkward revelation,
no well-meaning referral to how-to,
no reluctant embrace. only a series of reminders
too delightful to wish away,
too terrible to contemplate.

night of awe

    when under the caress of the impossible,
    the piers stretched long and dry
    and i was surrounded by sailor.
    they knew the paths to my exoneration.
    coats of whiteness gleamed over their hard thighs
    and my waiting mouth.
    their hats stayed perched,
    despite the oblivion of their thrust,
    in ways i could understand.
    those strange white hats!
    their hands were efficient with
    the exhaustion of my zipper
    and left reminders of my will to reverie.
    at some point, when all else slipped further,
    when it was only i under the sliver,
    i glimpsed new meaning in the verb "to moon."
    so this is what it meant.
    this was the reason for my coming.
    and still later, shivering under the thud,
    stumbling between stalks of needle,

pursued by laughter mocking my mincing step,
i came to pause by the cells of the other wayward.
through the bars of the gates, i found my way
to praise the stars
whose net of light was somehow able
to sustain this night,
the night of the first transgression.

don't relinquish glamour, child

    from nightly surprise
    these devout hands, of all hands,
    know the route of shorn hair.
    my knowledge can be condensed to this:
    use jelly for flattening, straightening, subduing.
    search my velvet case and find my mentor –
    the mother of all pearl.
    now, we will approach the wighead.
    what was, for me, a mere permissibility,
    perched somewhere between
    a legal concession to marital hunger
    and enforced modesty,
    will be your very crown of bravura.
    place the comb to the left.
    the curls must seem purposeful yet unplanned –
    like this.
    the frock you've chosen achieves its overall objective:
    black yet flapper, revealing yet elusive.
    include this beaded purse.
    no ensemble is complete without one. yes!

now tell me you've discovered the right shade;
virginia gooseberry is good.
turn around, no, slowly revolve under the shade
of my instruction:
let's see the face.
work with the cheek bones; never fight them.
these bones will be your salvation here.
remember that their lines will endure long after
your relentless beard has returned
and silenced the music and applause.

post parade ceremony: pride day, 199-

    we three not so sensitive boys,
    giddy and exhausted on the stench of liberation,
    could almost have been mellow
    after the spectacle of those so far
    from us to whom we had come to pay annual honor.
    this day could only foreshadow
    the grandeur of midsummer nights to come.
    today would soar into a monsoon of july mango.
    we knew this; we saw it.
    we felt it in the rivers of our knees.
    the knots of affiliation and place,
    the eccentricities of location – all this we beheld:
    the dim watering holes come to dry in the moist alley,
    corpses and effigies insisting through,
    boys and girls burning bold the costumes
    of their futures
    and the weight of mockery past …
    and so we hurried to spread tales
    of the day's abundance –
    the most devout, the most stout,

the most brave, the scantiest clad —
and yet, as always, we ended up with
the crowd favorites:
the elders who came and saw to stay.
etched on their placards were signs of struggle
and readings against exile.
not needing the details (there would be
time for that later),
we bowed only in honor of those who were there.
and of our own and others equally absent,
we pooled our spook and tried to conjure
their impossible attendance.

advice

look out for the one who sits at the front of the room,
with assignments crisp and complete.
who returns home with star and lunch
cauliflower consumed without cheek.
whom teachers, with voices drenched in echoes
of distant ambition,
caress for an ability to listen.

look out for the one who slips through
the web of congregants,
only occasionally remembered as a
blur at the ribs of the synagogue.
who reaches in the morning to greet
the challenges of God,
whom the rabbis pronounced safe
in the circle of the divine.

mothers, beware of the immensity of your expectation
and the fragility of your vigilance!

prediction: bowery yom kippur

       you will go to luminous spaces.
       on all nights sacred you will observe
       the hips of girls swallowed by insistent sound.
       powders and pills will reveal insight into time
       and plane and you will disappear into all
       that you have become.
       hard men whose torsos will gleam until you follow
       will hack apart thighs that will
       fall away in acceptance.
       troubadours wrapped in the tender stream of this
       deserving avenue will roar for their pittance
       and, on a hurricane of anxiety, you will sail.
       only know this: i won't be there.
       i will take leave of you at the cooper union.
       (into brown stone, an old woman will move.)
       but find the lines of my chill to glimpse
       all that you once knew.
       even only that.
       let that small search protect me from
       what my enstoned motherface
       will now always see:
       that an angel, disquieted, rides alone.

croquis in dust and shadow

we walked four sabbath mile to mother.
red flowers bloomed unnamed alongside.
in our stiff shoes and special dress, only dust rested.
father, all in black beneath the blaze,
impassive against the shouts of *heaholdmanheahrabbih
eahmotha***moses*,
expounded upon ethics.
mother, upon our arrival, spoke of the osmosis
of blandness
and the touch of her favorite nurse.
her spirits, we all agreed, seemed quite good.
before long, father called us for the
end-of-sabbath prayer.
afterwards, we all gathered by the window,
whispering each other a good week,
mother's roommate wheezing,
her shadow dancing on the curtain sealing her bed.

medical breakthrough

here, let me help you; your wig won't fall off.
let me undo your old bra; i won't mash your breasts.
my hands will only bring care.
i will make my way over the maps of blue
until i tear out the bruise and remains of needle.
i will study hard to uncover the route to relief.
with the advice of the most thorough engineers,
my levees will block the swell of your sugar.
in sudden fluency my tongue will revive
the sunken curve of your inner thigh.
and the men in white will be forced to take note.

the patriarch's power

as her body gradually emptied of parts,
the nights grew denser, better able to withstand
the ferocity of her screams that sought to shatter their
bravura. even the sobbing,
sometimes into the mattress,
sometimes into psalm,
which could once have trickled through fissures,
was met only by the still expectancy
of the night's emissaries.
only he could stay in the valley of death.
his beard swept over her thrashing remains and
brought her further into the cool center
of all that was allowed.
his words, echoes from the lives
of the saints and their wives,
helped her remember the grandeur of her choices.
only his big hands, his thick fingers
could satisfy the flesh burning beneath her scar·tissue.

current affairs

look at us, all pretense shredded.
scattered, adrift in resumption.
sometimes a sentence fraught with anxiety,
heavy with fear of the wrong verb.
occasionally an occasion or holiday.
words bulging under cheer.
perhaps something about a job.
(was it always this way?)
before, the eyes turned to your shuttered rooms.
now there's no wonder.
we know our roles:
supporting players milling about,
awaiting the entrance of the soloist.

culinary miracle

once i thought it would be easy.
that with time, poignant feasts could emerge.
if not roast chicken, then breaded fish.
if not spicy tsholnt, then perhaps vegetable soup.
if never family, then a small table of friends,
proud to sample the fruit of inspiration
gaining momentum.
once i thought that if i entered that room,
however cautiously,
if i just adjusted the flames to a manageable simmer,
i could make this ritual my own.

under linen trees, whispers

nothing ever diminished its hold.
the miles of sinew,
and yet the dip of the small,
a subtlety not to be missed, a detail so bold
and precise as to make me venture even
further into the erotic poem.
what was i thinking?
the miracle of my nipple
under the embrace of teeth.
my stubble (rrarr!) gathered on the rink
of your freshly shaved head.
the care of your cock guiding me
outside the dry thrust of speed and indifference.
as if for the first time …
for the first time!
so that nothing could have prepared me
for the framing of your forearm
against the hand stitching of the finest carolina linen,
a sudden vision of you with my matriarch
who would so have marveled

at your antebellum ancestor's eye,
who would have immediately understood
the clarity of its path.
and just as suddenly, this was all, all that was possible.
good man, a low and knotted land awaited us.
only we grew flushed and threatening
and fell back into clean and glittering retreat.

and from there to water

    i lay with giacomo on my narrow bed.
    today, he had put aside the legacy of his other
    (and i mine)
    and had come, between panels of downpour,
    past the pleasure of my italian landlady:
    in this flat land, her own dialect!
    from his sack emerged a thousand blue combs
    and barley soup grown cold. as the walls drew closer,
    giacomo said, eat this soup, this is what you need.
    about this, they could not have been wrong.
    though not from my village, he insisted,
    it's the same general idea.
    through the ozone, i saw his hands take my head,
    surrounding it with forearm.
    everything was how i imagined,
    even the mole below his left elbow.
    then he began to sing,
    a small number from the pulpit or the
    hard-to-find cabaret,
    telling stories in his impenetrable tongue.

in times like these,

he whispered, only my tongue.

but what would i remember,

how will i be sure, i wanted to know.

no response then,

only the march of what sounded like lilt and his

body trembling thin and hard beneath mine.

before and after introduction

there was nothing in the walk: a fine, loping gait.
how looking down, she noticed his coming toward,
his colors only just quieted by the fans
and the last stoop children of the day.
the shape of his work had lost
some of its oft-discussed flesh
so that some kind of line clung to his jaw.
this was apparent even from her protected
vantage point.
his hands, by his side, tended to remain there.
and his eyes and ears,
taut in the cocktail murmur,
also could be depended upon to stay.
and there were certainly no ditches, hardly a crevice.
the facade withstood the forces arrayed against it.
still, one could not shake the impression,
it was even in the trees around him,
the birches that had sprung up during
his trip to the punch bowl,
that something very grave had taken place.

implications of bread

his back is turned.
its precise route remains unclear.
that is: the stops of its travels, the early air gliders
unknown if not unimagined.
a book closed, a law flouted, a will steeled.
of course, this back cannot see how long
i have worked to allow
for a generosity to flower,
to point the way to decisions and meanings
to which i had longer committed myself.
to no avail but still you must know:
this embrace of exile that you see before you
now was not always so.
once was a young man who understood
the shimmer of the given,
the glow of giving way.
into the legalities came a light so white
it sometimes left me
a little breathless. you must know this.
this too is important.

but always was shared dough –
conceived in quiet wind, pummeled until bruised,
risen into gold and disguised.
not a world, but an entrance.
a door ajar.
this is where i stood; this was my perch.
needing no glasses, i gathered all my
front row privileges
to witness your inchoate bravado,
your wanderings into deviance and redemption.
here, i heard your calls for alliance and waited
and wait still.
my slow and sad revolutionary, my son,
you take fierce care.

II.

ARCHAEOLOGY OF SUGAR: METHODS

way of the footnote

i might take hold of pen, examine the clouds at hand.
scratch my chin,
contemplate the applicability of experience.
arrange the books on my desk to fulfill
some urgent symmetry.
i might pour a grapefruit juice
and think about the accretion of residue,
the peril of storage, the pleasure of hoarding.
i could also find some suitable clothes,
marvel at the fin-de-siècle dandy i have become.
i might nibble the pen,
contemplate the return of narrative verse
and the need to execute a certain parallel structure.
i might try to arrange the coils
and the ache around the edges of this poem
that threaten to reduce it to obscurity.

woman of letters

    sometimes i wish the sequence of things
    could have more closely
    resembled the corpus of the Delft master –
    a series of moments of contemplation,
    delicate with import.
    framed by pale glow and white marble,
    how could my days not have assumed a
    mantle of meaning?
    the sun flowing through the many diamond frames
    would have illuminated my letters from
    old friends and imagined beaus in warrens of anxiety.
    and i would have penned responses of
    hope and concern.
    i would have understood their need
    and the sweep of my stone rooms,
    suffused in the calm of northern light,
    would have eradicated their epistolary woe.

owning the terrain of detail

when our skin abraded on sight,
when we had to turn from the accusation
that rose opaque and succulent between us,
we tried other means.
here, we were sure, the pauses
would conceal our uncertainty.
distance would disguise our hunger for authority:

she used to knead so; this was
how the bread was formed.
a wooden rolling pin coated in flour always
stood near the green bowl.
i know this.

still, these details,
burdened under such import,
performed their own collective dance.
authenticity, desperately sought and just within reach,
hovered and then slipped away.
despite all our insistence

and the protection lent by our long-distance provider,
we knew that we hadn't gotten it quite right.

memorandum to the beleaguered graduate student

for Angelika Bammer

you must broaden the scope of your inquiry.
conduct fieldwork among cousins scattered
in walled enclaves
and the settlements outside the old old city, perhaps.
or forage in the archives of hospitals
strewn across continents
to uncover the records of ravage.
browse the photographs of the streets,
where the baker once knew her name.
pore over the social histories of park design
to see how a new arrangement of benches
could have changed everything.
how even the pigeons might have noticed.
in the accumulation of evidence provided
by the case study,
not the edifice imposed by the psychology text,
you will gain insight into the strategies of decay.
consult the international headlines or the theater obits

for some perspective, a sense of the times.
then you will assemble and tabulate your data,
(the reward for your labor in the
trenches of empiricism),
and bask in the smiles of your proud
and relieved dissertation committee.

women at the barricades

first he saw a hut swallowed by cloud,
then an underground cell, a gazebo,
finally a hill.
anything to avoid the urgency, the insistence
of these women whose acts he had
wandered to witness.
there could be no explanation for how it happened,
only an assertion that it did.
all he could do was sit on cliffs of velvet and marvel.
they did not merely appear;
they understood that there was a road
before them and behind.
yet they came in a strange procession
devoid of attachment and outside history.
one had tortoiseshell glasses and spoke
only of barricades and symbolist riddles.
a duo arrived in flowing robes
and invoked shadow figures heroic and slain.
he even glimpsed a group that had walked
with the disappeared.

together, all of them whispered to the young mother:
look at what we've done, take hold of your yearning.
they all warned that the hands
of empathy were fast closing
and that in their stead would be verse
of decorum and devotion.
he saw all this, he knows, he heard them,
he delivered their broadsides.
one of their champions, he broadcast
their hard-earned messages.
one of their admirers, he spoke of them,
in tones swift and unforgiving,
to ears deaf then unwilling.

in the attic, on the ocean floor

tipsy on half-understood theologies of liberation,
he once thought it would all become apparent.
one day, in the basement, beneath rotting pipes,
he would discover the jade:
perhaps a crate full of drawings of
street corners quickly understood
in the late morning shadow
or an all-knowing Catskills summer firefly,
designs of gowns with flair
or manuscripts of care and promise.
a moment of serendipity that could
have altered perception forever.
a moment that could have made
all this into something else.
one that would have expanded a narrow frame,
removed it from its own absence of expectation.
once he waited for the moment that
could have released a life
from the yoke of habit into the realm of deliverance.
silly boy!

notes from another tradition

path coated in bramble.
bloodied roses choke trellises.
a raccoon forages in ancient dumps.
weeds welcome the hope of grass.
behind curtain shreds leer wrinkled faces.
a woman rubs hand cream from the night
of her only dance.
from on high peals of non sequitur
give the mosquitoes pause.
he gathers all of these.
and looking over his shoulder,
he conceals them beneath his shirt
and scurries up the steps of the unraveling verandah.

red ink, white space

    these are compassionate encounters,
    said the professor in tones at once
    bohemian and tweedy.
    yours is an unwavering hand. but i'm looking for this.
    this is what i want to see:
    what is the relationship of the dissipation of flesh
    to the disappearance of vigor?
    in other words, which,
    if any, takes precedence?
    where is the location of origin?
    what must be etched are the decisions,
    the jitter of your subject's interiority and
    the actions that followed.
    i'm not looking for coherence
    or an assumption of persona
    but a means for navigating
    the unknowability of a life.
    as it stands, i see hints,
    richly suggestive. good.
    but if you're going to grapple effectively with the

essential laws of internal motion,
you will have to take us
from the discomfort of the threshold
and into the fertile dusk of these "dark rooms;"
you will have to remove the slipcovers
of the therapist's couch
and deliver us into the very heart of sorrow.

in the quick already gone

    when i remove my wig
    and you pretend not to see.
    when i brush with even strokes the floor
    cracks committed to historical preservation.
    when i turn beneath the bathroom glare
    the gray of my skirts ablaze.
    when i bend down to ease
    my ankles swollen in diligence,
    then, only then, will you begin to know.

the other woman

who is this harridan burdening these pages.
her shoulders bent, this obsession with headgear,
it's all off.
where is the woman who stood quiet
against the window.
did you see not see her pleasure
in the creation of order.
when the day opened, when she stood
with book in hand
and food on the way.
when God walked with her down
the weekly produce aisle.
when the understanding of queen esther's
resources dawned.
as your summers lengthened and her end
seemed ongoing,
her quiet was abandoned, discarded
for the wares of conflict seemingly more poetic.
this is how it looks.
but this other woman, she knows better.

she turns from the trajectory of descent,
rises from rest,
and continues the days of deed
and the life of commitment.

negotiation suspended

who granted this mantle,
bestowed the mask of authorial authority.
if there was a covenant, why was i not at the signing?
you could have paged me, at least.
you have my number.
unpack this a little further
and tell me what's there, child –
better uses and a future of solitary wine.
there are no answers; questions have evaporated –
years ago, after the war, perhaps.
the sympathy is misplaced; i have asked for none.
after years of pursuit,
bland finally before your pillaging,
i gather my basket of newly dried dates,
chew them with my usual gusto, and aim the pits
into the chasm at the center of these doggerel.

the earliest review

by us there has never been such a thing.
we have no need for such talk.
we speak small:
after seventy years,
a few words are gathered to remember
acts of generosity.
bread is given to a neighbor,
the destitute are sheltered.
we seek to give more to those to whom
we have already given.
after floundering, a greeting
in the darkening corridor,
with fresh linen and encouragement,
is extended.
words that help bring courage forth are offered.
and then with all this,
we refract our knowledge through words
greater than our own.
from memory we move into sanctity.
these are our ways.

only among the debased and the arrogant
could you have learned this other thing.
and i want no part in it.
if only on this one point, there cannot be ambiguity:
even in paying respect, you wreak devastation.

silk tabernacle

    these are the loves of my eternal partner.
    here we all assemble to bow our offerings
    and cry out.
    to you, master above.
    my requests are now so few.
    i ask primarily that you put aside your decrees
    for their brevity no longer brings me relief.
    from within the walls of these antechambers
    i see that exhaustion is not on your agenda
    and that your allies are gaining on me.
    the purpose of my actions is now beside the point.
    all that remains is their outcome:
    my place with the others,
    the gauze of my dreams around the corset
    of the millennium.

sandscape

      my face upon your psalm.
      water below a night lamp.
      perspiration into ice.
      a streak across a darkening courtyard.
      your voice outside my veil.

expanded empire

    remember me to the one who knew.
    drape me in hard clear beads.
    sever all ties to drudgery,
    release all obsession with melancholy.
    wrap me in mauve,
    on a throne of a thousand year reign.
    mine will be a smooth rule;
    no attention will be paid to the despots
    puffing behind the mirrors
    of my locked antechambers.
    affix a chiffon glow over the bird cages in my wigs.
    engrave me as the first lady of the shtetl
    and you my most trusted maidservant.

political funeral

they stood milling,
activists suspended in anticipation –
one foot and then the other.
certainly they had deliberated enough over this action.
into the night, long after the sub-subcommittees
had submitted
their final counterproposal.
the order they had sought was in the route of things,
where they would go,
how they would enact the passion
embedded within the finality of the mission at hand.
never mind, the time for surprise was over.
no drums now, only determination.
at the sign from the marshals,
they lifted the coffin high and began to march
down the cobblestone paths,
through the alleys ornate with silence,
the walls dense with disbelief.

by the grave: 'historian' and craft

    mother whispers to the gods,
    drawn by the warm circle of their indifference.
    the issues she raises, though not pressing,
    have a historical urgency, in their own way,
    a kind of politics of the absurd writ small.
    they have to do with causality:
    how were these clotted veins,
    this rising cost of sugar
    determined.
    subject motivation: that is, how can we, as remnants,
    get at reason, avoid the shoals of conjecture.
    what is the relationship of partisanship
    and subjectivity to the text at hand:
    a pain-wasted body, after all.
    this is not a popular history, remember.
    there are standards to be maintained.
    still, the central question of a benign divine
    has been dealt with,
    seems less important, anyway,
    given the news and the

newsreels.
let it go.
sleep, mother, sleep.

behind siesta eyes

don't think.
because the shutters are sealed
against the midday sun
and all the light in the heavens is bound outside
and only a single figure straggles through the dust
across the expanse of arches on its way
to a rendezvous of immediate clarification.
or that because the camera panning slowly
across the square
misses even this exception,
so absorbed in its study of line
and possible convergence.
or because the dogs, the ears of the dogs
have ceased to twitch
so spent are they by the fervor of the past week
of bread riot.
and that the girl, wandering from mirror to mirror,
is left wondering all this time why yellow
has been selected
as the color of hiding.

don't think,
don't think that just because of all this,
you aren't being seen and followed.

the unforsaken

beloved,
the prophets have not stopped their song.
they have refused to surrender memory's longing.
though the famines have left them uncertain –
food arranged in circles of inadequacy and rot,
emaciated bodies heeding their own worst fears,
stone staircases arching under cries
for assistance and imminent transgression –
they know all cannot be lost.
it has taken so long,
however, to acquire this knowledge.
everything will be done to ensure its longevity.
even the weak and the dying feel
certain of engagement.
a faith born of absence,
steady precisely because of disrepair,
is making itself visible.
the lowered torsos, the ebbing breath cannot
eradicate the ongoing focus.
beyond the facts of the shortages,

the array of crumbs,
unfold vast expanses of wheat and mystery.
here, the prophets know, is a likely arena
for their words.
pray for their work, pray that they succeed.
beloved.

GLOSSARY

gimnazye (Yiddish): European equivalent of high school

mikveh: ritual bath

Moishe Oysher (1907-1958): cantor, singer of liturgy and Yiddish song, actor

Mordechai Ben David: contemporary ultra-Orthodox pop star

néni (Hungarian): aunt

pogrom: organized massacre and looting of a minority group, especially Jews

Purim: Jewish holiday that celebrates the salvation of the Jews of the Persian Empire in the fifth century B.C.E. Led by Mordecai and Queen Esther, the Jews triumphed over Haman, who had plotted to destroy them. The holiday is celebrated with performance, costume, and revelry.

Queen Esther: Jewish heroine who saved the Jews from Haman's decree of destruction.

seder: Jewish home service on Passover, commemorating

chiefly the Jewish exodus from Egypt

sheytl (Yiddish): wig worn by Hasidic and Orthodox Jewish married women

shtetl: small Jewish town in Eastern Europe

shul: synagogue, school

talmudic: relating to, sharing characteristics of the Talmud, the two (Babylonian and Palestinian) collections of records of the discussion and administration of Jewish law during the period c. 200-500

tishah b'av: Jewish fast day commemorating the destruction of the temples in Jerusalem

tkhines (Yiddish): prayers, primarily for women

tsholnt (Yiddish): stew served on the Sabbath

Volozhin: town in Belarus (in Poland before 1793 and between 1921 and 1945), site of renowned yeshivah (academy of Jewish higher learning)

ACKNOWLEDGMENTS

I am profoundly indebted to the editors of the following publications in which these poems, sometimes in different form, first appeared or are scheduled to appear:

The Adirondack Review: "questions of dress"

Arlington Artsletter: "*tsholnt*"

Chiron Review: "scarcity"

Eclectica Magazine: "figure prostrate on tishah b'av stone" and "the filth box wreaks havoc!"

Erosha: "the last physical exam," "night of awe," and "under linen trees, whispers"

Evergreen Chronicles: "issue, hovering"

Fauquier Poetry Journal: "picnic withheld" and "retrenchment"

Free Verse: "woman of letters"

The Glass Cherry: "invasion"

Grasslands Review: "months that flu"

The James White Review: "by the grave: 'historian' and craft," "preparing to dance," "the question of moishe oysher"

Kinesis: "in the thermometer factory" and "the patriarch's power"

KotaPress Poetry Journal: "homage restored: bar mitzvah fantasia"

Lilliput Review: "culinary miracle"

Little Brown Poetry: "kindergarten blues"

Melic Review: "advice"

Muse Apprentice Guild: "still life, with mirrors," and "in praise of hope and honeydew"

Night Skye M.a.ga.z.i.n.e: "immigrant eyes, averted," "dust into stars," and "the way of the footnote"

Parnassus Literary Journal: "croquis in dust and shadow"

The Paumanok Review: "after theory" and "invitation to psalm"

Pearl: "eye contact"

Pierian Springs: "behind siesta eyes"

Pif Magazine: "iris outside time"

Poetic Inhalation: "caravaggio's latest boy," "identity confirmed," "implications of bread," "instead of school," and "other tongues (in case of flight)"

Poetry Daily: "*tsholnt*"

Prairie Schooner: "father grocer," "a house calling," and "*tsholnt*"

Queens College Journal of Jewish Studies: "despite virtue"

Response: "and from there to water"

Salt River Review: "arrangement without sun" and "dust into stars"

Samsara Quarterly: "medical breakthrough"

Snakeskin: "east central european paradigms"

(this) poetry site: "don't relinquish glamour, child"

Tsukunft: Yiddish version of "preparing to dance"

ADDITIONAL CREDITS

The poems which appeared in *Prairie Schooner* were reprinted in *The Prairie Schooner Anthology of Contemporary Jewish American Writing* (University of Nebraska Press, 1998).

"Questions of dress" was nominated by *The Adirondack Review* for the Pushcart Prize.

My thanks to Brukhe Lang Caplan, who edited the Yiddish version of "preparing to dance."

Erin McGonigle provided an early audience for some of these poems and offered support and insightful feedback. Angelika Bammer intervened at a critical juncture; the effects of that intervention remain. Pearl Gluck has been an advocate for this project and a rigorous friend. Numerous conversations with Laura S. Levitt over the years have helped me imagine the second part of this book. Laura's vision and generosity of spirit continue to inspire. I am especially grateful to Katherine Arline of Wind River Press for her belief in my work and for gracefully shepherding the manuscript to publication.

In ways direct and indirect, the following individuals furthered the completion of this book: Dana Bialow, Hinde Ena Burstin, Richard (Zishe) Carlow, Olga Dugan, Nancy Emery, Mary Ann Farrior, Krysia Fisher, Ken Giese, Erica Kaplan, Esther Kaplan, Joan Leggett, James Meyer, Christopher Murray, Chana Pollack, Norma Fain Pratt, Scott Rednour, Jenny Romaine, Yankl Salant, Paul Edward Schaper, Melanie Search, Ronda Shiff, Donna Smith, and Roland Tec. Thank you all.

ABOUT THE AUTHOR

 A native of Philadelphia, Yermiyahu Ahron Taub is a Phi Beta Kappa and summa cum laude graduate of Temple University. He holds an M.A. in history from Emory University and an M.L.S. from Queens College, City University of New York. He lives in Washington, DC.

ABOUT THE PRESS

Founded in 2001, Wind River Press of Hershey, Pennsylvania publishes the literary magazine *The Paumanok Review,* the critical review *Critique* in addition to select electronic and trade paperback titles for the world audience. Wind River Press strives to take advantage of new and emerging technologies while embracing timeless standards of quality.

http://www.windriverpress.com